ABLAZE
~with
COLOR
A STORY OF PAINTER
ALMA THOMAS

WRITTEN BY JEANNE WALKER HARVEY

ILLUSTRATED BY LOVEIS WISE

HARPER
An Imprint of HarperCollinsPublishers

Former president Barack Obama's words at a White House
event honoring Black History Month in 2015:

Now, as always, this month is a chance to celebrate the central
role that African Americans have played in every aspect
of American life. . . . And here at the White House, we're
committed to honoring that legacy. Earlier this month . . .
we opened up the newly restored Old Family Dining Room . . .
and it now includes a painting by Alma Thomas called
Resurrection—and that's the first in the White House Collection
by an African American woman. [First Lady] Michelle made
that happen, and we could not be prouder. . . .

—Courtesy Barack Obama Presidential Library

I dedicate this book to my wonderful sons, Scott and Will.
And with heartfelt thanks to editor extraordinaire Megan Ilnitzki, agent extraordinaire
Deborah Warren, and the HarperCollins team: Chelsea C. Donaldson, art director;
Caitlin Stamper, designer; and Shona McCarthy, copy editor. —JWH

This book is dedicated to my four favorite matriarchs: Arnita, Elnora, Toni, and Martina.
Thank you for your constant inspiration, creativity, and dreams. —LW

Ablaze with Color: A Story of Painter Alma Thomas · Text copyright © 2022 by Jeanne Walker Harvey · Illustrations copyright
© 2022 by Loveis Wise · All rights reserved. Printed in the United States of America · No part of this book may be used or reproduced in
any manner whatsoever without written permission except in the case of brief quotations embodied in critical articles and reviews.
For information address HarperCollins Children's Books, a division of HarperCollins Publishers, 195 Broadway, New York, NY
10007 · www.harpercollinschildrens.com · Library of Congress Control Number: 2021933141 · ISBN 978-0-06-302189-1
The artist used Adobe Photoshop to create the digital illustrations for this book · Typography by Chelsea C. Donaldson
23 24 25 PC 10 9 8 7 6 5 4 3 ❖ First Edition

Through color, I have sought to concentrate on beauty and happiness, rather than on man's inhumanity to man. —Alma Thomas (1970)

Alma always felt her best
when she was outside soaking up
the sparkling colors of nature.
In the garden at her house on a hill,
she skipped around circles of flowers.
Pastel purple violets and crimson roses
crowned by bright green banana leaves.

She fell back on the grass
beneath poplar trees
and gazed at quivering yellow leaves
that whistled in the wind.
Alma waded in the blue hues of a brook
and basked in the warm glow of sunsets.

Alma was always on the go,
never wanting to sit or cook or sew
like her three younger sisters.
She wanted to make things,
things that she could hold.

Alma scooped up moist red clay
from the banks of the nearby stream.
She shaped small bowls and cups
to dry in the sizzling sun.

Inside her house, Alma's world
was also full of color and creativity.
Her mother designed dazzling dresses,
singing as she sewed.
Her aunts painted petals and patterns,
and Alma dipped her brush in tiny pots.

Although Alma felt joy at home,
she and her sisters were sad
they couldn't attend the school
just two doors away,
the white school.
And they couldn't enter museums
or the town library.

So Alma's parents filled their home with books and created their own place of learning.

They invited teachers into their living room to talk
about people and places around the world,
famous stories, and ways of thinking.
Even though Alma didn't understand
all that was said by the grown-ups,
she watched and listened.

When Alma turned fifteen
and couldn't attend the local high school,
her family decided to move to the North.
Away from the injustices of the South.

After the train crossed the state border,
Alma's mother told her girls to take off their shoes
and shake out the Georgia sand.
And never go back again.

The family moved into a house
in Washington, DC,
where Alma would live
for most of her life.

A house with a flower garden,
a patch of nature
that always made her happy.

When Alma grew up,
she studied art in college.
She chose to share her love of art
by teaching at the local school.

But even in the nation's capital,
schools were still segregated
and access to art limited.

Alma was determined to bring art
to the young in her neighborhood.
Just as her parents had brought learning
into her home when she was young.

Alma invited children into her living room
and taught them to make wooden marionettes.
They performed their own plays
when they weren't allowed
to see puppet shows downtown.

In her free time, Alma painted, studied,
and shared ideas with artist friends.
Sometimes their work was exhibited together.

Mainly, though, she devoted herself to helping children,
leading field trips and art clubs
and setting up the city's first gallery in a school.

Finally, when Alma was almost seventy years old,
she stopped teaching and focused on her own art.

Sitting in her favorite red chair,
she stared at the patterns of light and color
twinkling through the leaves of her holly tree.
Just as she had watched the fluttering leaves
of the poplar trees when she was a young girl.

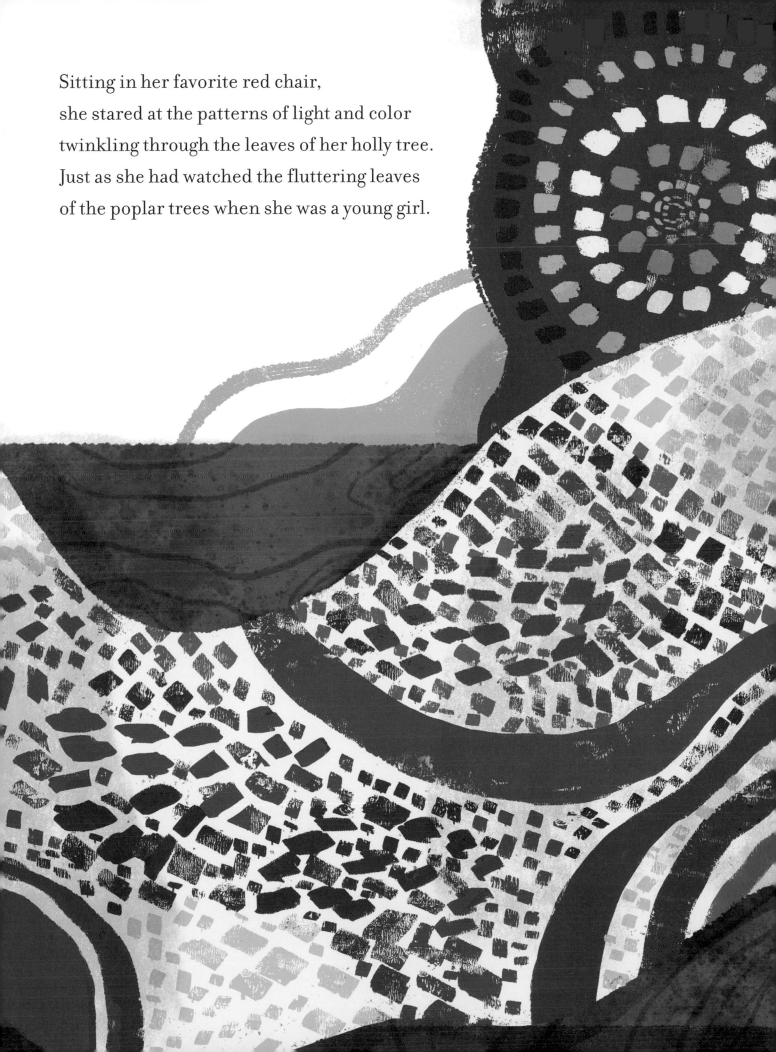

Inspired by what she saw,
Alma began painting in a new style.
Circles and stripes.
Dashes and dabs.
Ablaze with color.
Soft colors, bright colors.

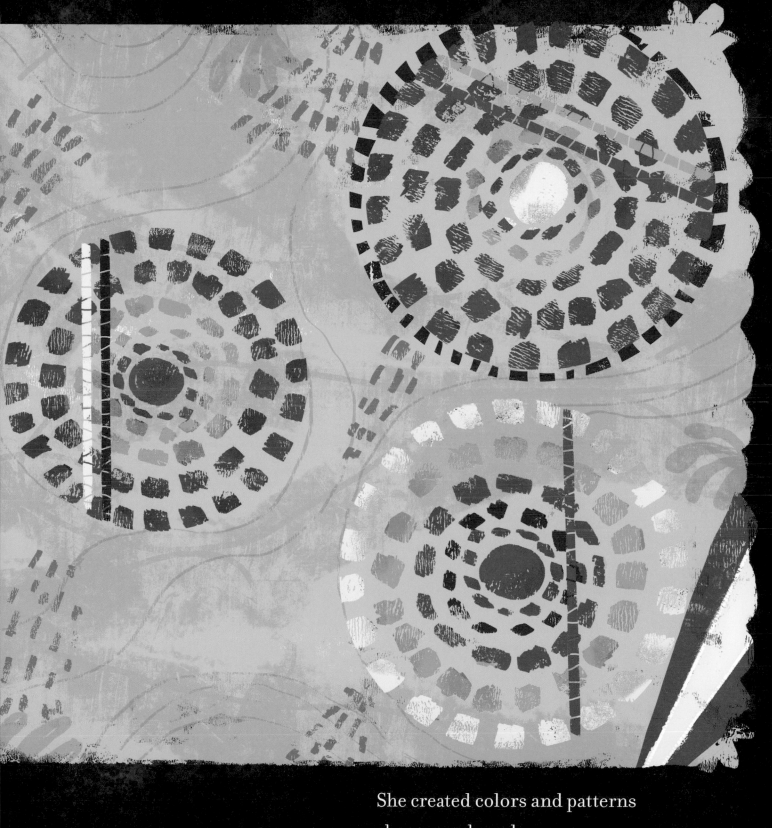

She created colors and patterns

she remembered

from her childhood days in the South

and from what she saw now

She painted how she felt on the inside
when she experienced nature outside.
The wind.
The sunshine.
The flowers.
How nature made her heart sing and dance,
even when life could be hard and unjust.

Alma imagined soaring high in an airplane,
even though she had never been in one.
Gardens and trees below
became streaks and smudges.

Amazed by space travel, new at the time,
Alma envisioned traveling aboard
rockets with astronauts.
The starry sky and zooming spaceships
glimmered as dashes and swatches.

Galleries began showing Alma's new artwork.
And then . . . the unexpected happened.

The Whitney, a famous art museum in New York City,
featured Alma's *Paintings of Earth and Space*.
The first solo show by a Black woman.

Thrilled by the honor, Alma greeted crowds
gathered at the museum,
a place where everyone could visit.

Later that year, the Corcoran Gallery of Art,
a large museum in DC,
also showcased her paintings.
The mayor proclaimed September 9
as "Alma Thomas Day"
to celebrate Alma, her art,
and all she had done for the city's youth.

Sadly, Alma didn't live
to see the momentous day—

when the first Black president and First Lady
chose Alma's painting
as the first artwork by a Black woman
to be displayed in the White House,
the home of the president's family
and a symbol of the American people.

Alma's art shimmered above a long table
in the Old Family Dining Room of the White House,
where famous leaders, teachers, and artists gathered.
Just as people had gathered
in Alma's childhood home.
Just as children had gathered
in Alma's DC house.

In Alma's piece,
yellow dashes twirl.
Circles upon circles swirl.

Orange
Red
Purple
Blue

A soft, quiet center,
a green of nature.

A painting of hope
and joy.
Ablaze with glorious color.

ALMA'S COLORS.

AUTHOR'S NOTE

When I learned that Alma Woodsey Thomas's 1966 abstract painting, titled *Resurrection*, was chosen as the first artwork by a Black woman to be added to the White House permanent collection, I immediately knew I wanted to share Alma's exceptional life and art by writing a children's book about her. Former first lady Michelle Obama explained that she and former president Barack Obama, the first Black US president, chose contemporary art because they believed "life in the White House could be forward leaning without losing any of its established history and tradition."[1]

I greatly admire Alma's dedication to both of her careers, as an arts educator for children and as an artist. Despite the challenges of discrimination, she approached her life with the conviction that "we can't accept any barriers, any limitations of any kind, on what we create or how we do it."[2]

Alma often explained that "the use of color in my paintings is of paramount importance to me."[3] She believed "colors are the children of light" and light reveals "the spirit and living soul of the world."[4]

Whenever I see Alma's artwork, my spirits are lifted. I'm deeply grateful that I had the opportunity to write about her inspiring life and paintings, ablaze with joyous color.

Portrait of Alma Thomas, 1971. Photograph © by Ida Jervis. Courtesy Margaret L. Jervis and Anacostia Community Museum/Smithsonian Institution.

ILLUSTRATOR'S NOTE

Alma's harmonious work expresses the way we imagine beauty and joy through vibrancy. Like her, I believe that through color we discover our own inner truth, liberation, and happiness.

Blast Off by Alma Thomas, acrylic on canvas, 1970. Gift of Vincent Melzac, Smithsonian National Air and Space Museum (NASM) Collection.

White House Old Family Dining Room featuring *Resurrection* by Alma Thomas, acrylic and graphite on canvas, 1966. Courtesy Barack Obama Presidential Library. Official White House Photo by Amanda Lucidon.

TIMELINE

Alma's lifetime spanned enormous political, cultural, and scientific changes. As she said, "I was born at the end of the nineteenth century, horse-and-buggy days, and experienced the phenomenal changes of the twentieth-century machine and space age."[5]

ALMA'S LIFE

Born in Columbus, Georgia, on September 22. — **1891**

Family moves to DC. — **1907**

Graduates from Armstrong Manual Training School. — **1911**

Teaches children in Maryland, Delaware, and DC. — **1913–1923**

Receives Howard University's first undergraduate degree in fine arts. — **1924**

Begins teaching art at Shaw Junior High School in DC.

Receives master's degree in education at Columbia University. — **1934**

Leads the School Arts League Project for African American children in DC. — **1936–1939**

EVENTS IN THE UNITED STATES

1896 — US Supreme Court rules racial segregation constitutional. Jim Crow laws ("separate but equal") begin, barring Black Americans from equal access to public facilities.

1903 — The Wright Brothers fly first engine-powered airplane.

1906 — During the Atlanta, Georgia, race riot, white mobs attack Black citizens.

1916–1970 — During "the Great Migration," more than six million Black Americans move from the South to the North, Midwest, and West to seek better lives.

1917 — The United States enters World War I.

1941 — The United States enters World War II.

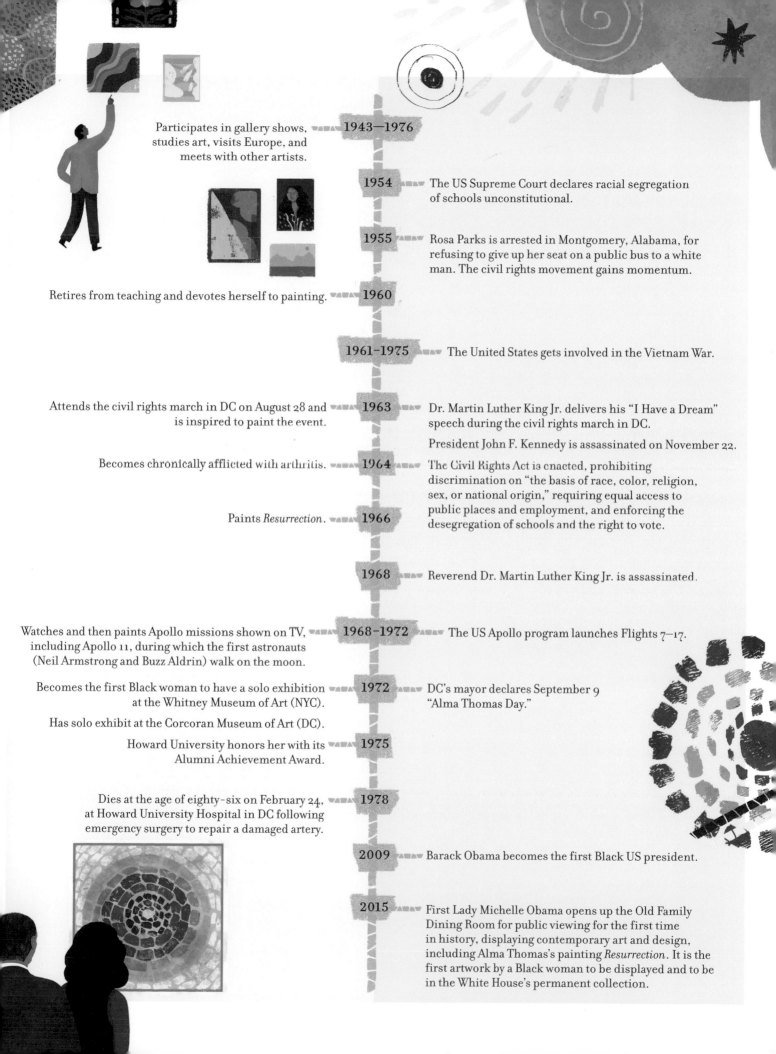

Participates in gallery shows, studies art, visits Europe, and meets with other artists. ◄▬▬ **1943–1976**

1954 ▬▬► The US Supreme Court declares racial segregation of schools unconstitutional.

1955 ▬▬► Rosa Parks is arrested in Montgomery, Alabama, for refusing to give up her seat on a public bus to a white man. The civil rights movement gains momentum.

Retires from teaching and devotes herself to painting. ◄▬▬ **1960**

1961–1975 ▬▬► The United States gets involved in the Vietnam War.

Attends the civil rights march in DC on August 28 and is inspired to paint the event. ◄▬▬ **1963** ▬▬► Dr. Martin Luther King Jr. delivers his "I Have a Dream" speech during the civil rights march in DC.

President John F. Kennedy is assassinated on November 22.

Becomes chronically afflicted with arthritis. ◄▬▬ **1964** ▬▬► The Civil Rights Act is enacted, prohibiting discrimination on "the basis of race, color, religion, sex, or national origin," requiring equal access to public places and employment, and enforcing the desegregation of schools and the right to vote.

Paints *Resurrection*. ◄▬▬ **1966**

1968 ▬▬► Reverend Dr. Martin Luther King Jr. is assassinated.

Watches and then paints Apollo missions shown on TV, including Apollo 11, during which the first astronauts (Neil Armstrong and Buzz Aldrin) walk on the moon. ◄▬▬ **1968–1972** ▬▬► The US Apollo program launches Flights 7–17.

Becomes the first Black woman to have a solo exhibition at the Whitney Museum of Art (NYC). ◄▬▬ **1972** ▬▬► DC's mayor declares September 9 "Alma Thomas Day."

Has solo exhibit at the Corcoran Museum of Art (DC).

Howard University honors her with its Alumni Achievement Award. ◄▬▬ **1975**

Dies at the age of eighty-six on February 24, at Howard University Hospital in DC following emergency surgery to repair a damaged artery. ◄▬▬ **1978**

2009 ▬▬► Barack Obama becomes the first Black US president.

2015 ▬▬► First Lady Michelle Obama opens up the Old Family Dining Room for public viewing for the first time in history, displaying contemporary art and design, including Alma Thomas's painting *Resurrection*. It is the first artwork by a Black woman to be displayed and to be in the White House's permanent collection.

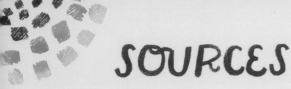

SOURCES

Museum Websites Featuring Alma Thomas

The Columbus Museum, Columbus, Georgia
https://columbusmuseum.pastperfectonline.com
/bycreator?keyword=Thomas,+Alma+Woodsey
This museum is in Alma Thomas's hometown and
includes an extensive collection of her paintings
and papers, including her marionettes.

**The Studio Museum in Harlem,
New York, New York**
https://studiomuseum.org/exhibition/alma-thomas
Website highlights the 2016 exhibition of Alma
Thomas's art.

National Gallery of Art, Washington, DC
www.nga.gov/collection/artist-info.1926.html

**National Museum of Women in the Arts,
Washington, DC**
www.nmwa.org/art/artists/alma-woodsey-thomas

**Smithsonian American Art Museum,
Washington, DC**
www.americanart.si.edu/artist/alma-thomas-4778

**The Frances Young Tang Teaching Museum and
Art Gallery at Skidmore College**
https://tang.skidmore.edu/exhibitions/133-alma-thomas

NOTES

1. Michelle Obama, *Becoming* (New York: Crown, 2018),
   309.
2. Adolphus Ealey, "Remembering Alma" in *A Life in
   Art: Alma Thomas*, 1891–1978, Merry A. Foresta, ed.
   (Washington, DC: Smithsonian Institution Press
   for the National Museum of American Art, 1981),
   exhibition catalog.
3. H. E. Mahal, "Interviews: Four Afro-American
   Artists: Approaches to Inhumanity." *Art Gallery* 13,
   no. 7 (April 1970): 36–37.
4. Alma Thomas Papers, ca 1894–2001, Archive
   of American Art, Smithsonian Institution,
   Washington, DC.
5. Alma Thomas Artist Statement, 1972, p. 216 in *Alma
   Thomas* by Ian Berry and Lauren Hayes.
   (See reference in Adult Books section)

REFERENCES

Articles

Allman, William. "Old Family Dining Room,
   Made New Again," February 10, 2015, https://
   obamawhitehouse.archives.gov/blog/2015/02/10/old
   -family-dining-room-made-new-again.
Munro, E. "The Late Spring Time of Alma Thomas," *The
   Washington Post*, April 15, 1979, www.washingtonpost
   .com/archive/lifestyle/magazine/1979/04/15/the
   -late-spring-time-of-alma-thomas/f205cbf7-3483
   -4cc4-8a52-7f5eacda7925.
Shirey, David L. "At 77, She's Made It to the Whitney."
   The New York Times, May 4, 1972, www.nytimes
   .com/1972/05/04/archives/at-77-shes-made-it-to
   -the-whitney.html.

Children's Books

Etinde-Crompton, Charlotte, and Samuel Willard
   Crompton. *Alma Woodsey Thomas: Painter and
   Educator.* Berkeley Heights, NJ: Enslow Publishing,
   2019. (Ages 12–17)
Ignotofsky, Rachel. *Women in Art: 50 Fearless Creatives
   Who Inspired the World.* New York: Ten Speed Press,
   2019. (Ages 10 and up)

Adult Books

Berry, Ian, and Lauren Hayes, *Alma Thomas.* New
   York: Delmonico Books, 2016. (A comprehensive
   monograph in connection with the exhibits at the
   Studio Museum in Harlem and the Frances Young
   Tang Teaching Museum and Art Gallery at Skidmore
   College)
Thomas, Alma Woodsey, and Fort Wayne Museum of
   Art. *Alma W. Thomas: A Retrospective of the Paintings.*
   San Francisco: Pomegranate, 1998. (Exhibition
   catalog for the traveling exhibit organized by the Fort
   Wayne Museum of Art)